OXFORD AND SOUTH MIDLAND BUSES

MATT COOPER

AMBERLEY

First published 2022

Amberley Publishing
The Hill, Stroud
Gloucestershire, GL5 4EP

www.amberley-books.com

Copyright © Matt Cooper, 2022

The right of Matt Cooper to be identified as
the Author of this work has been asserted in
accordance with the Copyrights, Designs and
Patents Act 1988.

ISBN 978 1 3981 1118 9 (print)
ISBN 978 1 3981 1119 6 (ebook)

British Library Cataloguing in Publication Data.
A catalogue record for this book is available from
the British Library.

Typesetting by Hurix Digital, India.
Printed in Great Britain.

Introduction

Visiting Oxford in the late 1980s and 1990s was always fascinating. A busy and bustling environment with buses and coaches appearing from every angle, a notepad was easily filled with fleet numbers and information. What happened in Oxford was a working example of the vision the government of the day had when privatisation of the industry was announced in the 1985 Transport Act. The city had the right environment for deregulation to work with several factors contributing to this. A very proactive council favoured public transport and from the early 1970s had invested in good infrastructure for bus companies to use, the trade-off being they would utilise it at their own expense with little or no subsidy. Part of this investment was the UK's first park and ride service offering the motorist easy access to the city centre without clogging it up. Central car park prices were kept high as a deterrent.

The National Bus Company (NBC) had united the operations of City of Oxford Motor Services (COMS) and that of South Midland to form Oxford South Midland in 1973. With deregulation in the air the two were split once more, South Midland even introducing a number of new fleet liveries on the run-up to privatisation. Both divisions were some of the first sold by NBC, number nine being South Midland, sold to a management buyout in December 1986. Despite five interested parties there was only one bid. COMS, however, had nine interested parties with three bids made. The management buyout was successful in January 1987, marking NBC's fourteenth sale. Stagecoach Holdings was one such interested party but for the time being would only serve the university city on routes from the north and west through other company acquisitions. This position would, of course, change.

Devon General had been the first NBC company to be sold to a management buy-out in August 1986, led by Harry Blundred (later OBE). Eager to get a piece of the action in Oxford, where Harry had worked during NBC days, Thames Transit was launched on 7 March 1987. Initial operations were one city route, using Mellor-bodied Ford Transits, and 'The Oxford Tube' coach service to London. Expansion would soon follow using the Exeter ethos and high-frequency minibus services served the city from all directions. By late 1988 the routes and vehicles of South Midland were acquired with Transit Holdings' unique style soon applied. This made for an interesting operation with a different outlook. Most routes were 'named' and vehicles didn't carry third party advertising, its own strong branding taking centre stage. Centre exits were a must, even on the minibuses. The phrase 'Way Ahead' was displayed on vehicles and in publicity, pointing to a time when things were described as 'way cool'. 'Investor in People' awards and ISO 9000 accolades were achieved and drivers could also proudly wear 'PSV badges' displaying the fictitious area code TT. This determined competitor fought its corner and made its own mark on the city's transport scene. Its legacy is very much in evidence today with 'turn up and go' 24-hour operation on city and rural routes and passenger numbers the envy of most comparable towns and cities.

Competition countered complacency and COMS responded accordingly to this new company, marketing itself as Oxford Bus Company. After some initial jostling both organisations quickly settled down to provide the travelling public of Oxford and the surrounding area some fantastic travel options together with well-priced ticketing. For example, £830 in 2001 would buy you an annual Freedom pass for use on all COMS services including coach routes. This also provided competition with rail services at the time, and commuter coaches remained very popular.

The Oxford to London corridor was also ground fiercely contested. While at COMS Harry Blundred was involved with this route becoming a 'shuttle' service with its own distinctive branding and livery. Risque advertising at the time stated 'Citylink 190 drivers do it every half hour', which now seems somewhat dated and more akin to a *Carry On* film. After some teething troubles the Oxford Tube service went on to be a great success. The initial Tube frequency of half-hourly progressively increased and both operators went on to run coaches twenty-four hours a day with departures up to every twelve minutes at peak times. Friendly, competitive banter from ticket-selling staff on the stand at Gloucester Green was always good to observe. One of Europe's most frequent intercity coach services, today the route is solely in the hands of Stagecoach's Oxford Tube, COMS withdrawing the X90 in January 2020.

Park and ride is a major part of the city's transport scene and was the UK's first such operation when launched in 1973. COMS has been the principal operator serving the four (later five) main car park sites, with vehicles allocated to such work carrying dedicated branding and a different livery style to the main fleet. Drivers migrated to this rota, and the use of 'kerb-siders' collecting fares during busy periods could be seen both in the city centre and at the car parks. In 1997 a total of 3,800 parking spaces were on offer at sites located at main compass points served by two frequent cross-city routes. Operating between 5 a.m. and midnight, a twelve-trip ticket could be purchased for £5. Thames Transit ran in competition on the north–south route until 1996 using minibuses. Other routes were later created linking car parks to destinations such as John Radcliffe Hospital and the Thornhill site utilised by passing coach services to London and its airports.

By the mid-1990s both of the city's main operators were owned by the industry's PLCs. In March 1994 COMS passed to the Go-Ahead Group, which soon applied three brands for city, coach and park and ride operations. Some 'cage rattling' took place with the still independent Thames Transit, which launched the 'Heathrow Tube' coach service and additional city services to some areas that only COMS served. This route retaliation came in response to 'Cityline' express routes to Abingdon and Bicester. Very reasonably priced fares were lowered still further in 1996 with, for example, the London day return fare becoming £2.97.

Shortly after celebrating their first decade of service in the city, in July 1997 Transit Holdings sold TT to the Stagecoach Group for £8.3 million. Innovation and quality would remain the hallmarks under both operators' new owners and the age profile of their fleets was kept low by frequent deliveries of new vehicles.

The expanding Stagecoach Group took the opportunity to merge some operations in the area from the late 1990s into a new division named Stagecoach South Midlands. This reincarnation of the name was not displayed publicly, each unit retaining fleet names of Stagecoach Midland Red and Stagecoach Oxford. The low-cost coach service Megabus was also launched under the division's control in 2003. A year later operations were split once more with Oxfordshire and the Oxford Tube run under its own control. Stagecoach in Warwickshire took most of the former Midland Red depots, with its Rugby head office also becoming the hub of Megabus UK and European services. This coach division was very flexible with routes being launched and developed as opportunities were presented.

While in Warwickshire we meet the operations of West Midlands Travel. This former PTE company was privatised as one whole unit in 1991 and holds a significant presence in the West Midlands conurbation. Companies wishing to carve their own niche must offer something unique, as was the case with the Diamond Bus operation, run by Go-Ahead Group under Oxford's control between 2004 and 2008.

Our journey will take us around the city of Oxford and into some areas of the county. The vague geographical term of 'South Midlands' has been used liberally in this book and certain operations in Northamptonshire and Warwickshire are featured. We will see cross-county coach services, some with the destination of Cambridge, which have played a significant role in linking the two cities. More recently, rail links through the county towards the capital have greatly improved and the 'permanent way' re-established on the Varsity Line.

The period covered by this book will highlight the positive effects of privatisation and the competitive environment it created that acted as a catalyst for innovation, new technologies and good marketing as well as an excellent service being offered to the public. Unconventional and intuitive theories were applied by both of Oxford's main bus operators. In the 1980s passengers boarding COMS or Thames Transit vehicles received their tickets from electronic ticket machines, technology which the operators could use behind the scenes to analyse passenger flows. COMS had an early presence on the internet with details displayed on vehicles as early as 1997. At the forefront of environmental policies, low-emission vehicles were specified from the early 1990s, although grand plans for a guided bus network didn't come to fruition. Towards the end of the chapter, in March 2010, the scene had evolved when Stagecoach Oxford, COMS and Oxfordshire County Council entered into an agreement to co-ordinate services, introduce joint ticketing and eliminate wasteful competition.

This snapshot of the era aims to show the rapid changes occurring at that time, which shaped the scene existing today. I have tried to include as many operators and vehicle types as possible but sadly couldn't cover them all. A lot changed in a relatively short space of time and I hope memories will be evoked by the scenes portrayed in this book. For ease, the term COMS has been applied to references made to that company, as a number of identities and brand names were used during this period. While conducting research I was amazed how many postcards ended up in my collection that prominently feature period buses with the backdrop of historic city buildings. Were they intended for use by tourists who perhaps wrote 'Dear Great Aunt Mavis, here in sunny Oxford, just had a trip on a COMS Gardner-engined Leyland Olympian and one of Harry's beloved Ford Transits'?!

My grateful thanks are due for the photographic assistance of Raymond Bedford, Colin Lloyd, Rob Edworthy, Nigel Wheeler, R. Eversden and Kevin Lane. There are some other unattributed shots which I've chosen from my collection. Thanks also to Bob Jackson for the proofreading and advice, and to Connor Stait and the staff at Amberley Publishing for taking on the project. Most importantly I am indebted to my wife and family for their support, help, understanding and patience throughout this book's creation.

With the music of Barrington Pheloung playing in the distance, lets head to Gloucester Green or Carfax with notepads and fleet books at the ready, and begin our journey.

Background and History

Since 1935 Gloucester Green has been the hub of coach and interurban services. In this mid-1970s scene a trio of single-deckers are sandwiched between platforms 1 and 2. The AEC on the right, with the furthest distance to travel, still wears City of Oxford Motor Services (COMS) red, maroon and duck egg green livery with NBC corporate fleet names applied. The Ford in the centre, one of twenty-one similar vehicles bodied by Willowbrook, will only work part way to Wootton, the destination of Chipping Norton being the full route. Winding its way to Thame on the 74A via Horspath, Wheatley and Shabbington was another AEC, this time in dual-purpose livery. Suffix letters featured on numerous routes at this time. (Author's collection)

Oxford has enjoyed excellent links by coach to London and its airports. One of five Plaxton Paramount 3500-bodied Leyland Tigers delivered in 1984 featured 'Bus Grant' doors, and stands at Gloucester Green when brand new. Wearing NBC's 'Venetian blind' livery, the comfortable seating will be appreciated by passengers heading to Heathrow. After ten years at Oxford further airport duties followed when this coach and two others of the batch were transferred to fellow company Wycombe Bus for their X80 'Heathrow Direct' from Aylesbury, Wycombe and Marlow launched in April 1994. It was later sold to Bennetts of Chievely and then Heyfordian. (Author's collection)

A complete refurbishment of Gloucester Green took place in 1989. With new flats, offices and retail outlets added, the bus station's smaller footprint would test a driver's manoeuvrability skills. Part of the 'old school' can be seen at the top left; its use has varied from bus company offices, waiting room, tourist office and now a restaurant and pub. The main feature of the picture is Stagecoach Oxford's Transbus Dart/Pointer 34466 (KV53 NHA) – the first of a batch of seven. One of a limited number of bus services to use the facility, Stagecoach Group vehicles dominate this 2 June 2008 scene.

Having traditionally been users of AECs and Daimler Fleetlines between 1973 and 1981, the standard COMS double-decker became the ECW-bodied Bristol VR. Single- and dual-door examples were delivered with 476 (HUD 476S) representing the latter. Originally to be numbered 926 when delivered in 1978 it became the 'Centenary bus' in 1981, celebrating 100 years of public transport in Oxford. A traditional livery was applied and a Transign electronic destination blind was also fitted at that time. It retained this livery for the remainder of its working life and is now part of the Oxford Bus Museum collection as shown here at that organisation's Long Hanborough site on 22 May 1998 during their Bristol VR day.

Winding the clock forward twenty-five years, two of Oxford Bus Company's Wright Renown-bodied Volvo B10BLEs received traditional liveries for the 125th year celebrations. The 'bus' version was carried well on 816's modern lines, viewed setting down passengers at Carfax while working its regular route 5 – whereas 817 received a Tramways-themed livery. (Author's collection)

In March 1987 Thames Transit launched a city route to Blackbird Leys using sixteen-seat Ford Transits bodied by Mellor. Other routes soon followed, with forty-two of the type eventually being used. At Bure Place bus station in October 1994 Ford Transit 104 waits together with the slightly larger Mercedes-Benz 709D bodied by Reeve Burgess. Hail & Ride vinyls are displayed on both vehicles; this was a major selling feature of the company. The acquisition of South Midland in 1988 gave TT a presence in surrounding towns such as Bicester. (Author's collection)

The Oxford Tube was also launched on 7 March 1987 using coaches transferred from Exeter. Initially operating a thirty-minute frequency to the London terminus at Marble Arch, after some early teething problems the service would develop to become a very worthy and innovative rival to the established Citylink service. Formerly with the Greenslades coaching unit as 2212, B402 UOD was a Duple Laser-bodied Leyland Tiger, one of six used from 1987 along with two Plaxton-bodied examples. Awaiting its move from the south-west to Oxford in its new livery, but lacking vinyls, the coach would receive fleet number 5 but no college name. (Rob Edworthy/ Author's collection)

City Scenes

Picking up on a very quiet Cornmarket Street is 512 (PFC 512W) of COMS' final batch of Bristol VRs working cross-city to Kidlington from Barton. Carrying a local overall advert for The Oxford Story, such liveries at this time were hand-painted. This May 1988 view also illustrates the use of 'Oxford Bus Company' as the fleet name. A Carlyle-bodied Ford Transit wearing 'Nipper' colours waits behind. COMS was an early recipient of minibuses for city services with the 'luxury' of long wheelbase units and twenty seats. (Author's collection)

London Buses began large-scale withdrawal of its Leyland Titan 'T' class from 1993 with this quirky and complex type finding new homes all over the UK. COMS chose them to replace Bristol VRs from the end of 1993 following successful use of a demonstrator that April. A more typical scene of Cornmarket Street and a health and safety department's worst nightmare, buses and pedestrians would remain in partnership on this thoroughfare until 1999. In 1994 KYV 392X, formerly T392 and now numbered 967, is devoid of fleet names as it works towards Kidlington. (Author's collection)

Freshly painted and looking resplendent 965 (OHV 783Y), ex-T783, was being driven by engineering staff in this November 1993 view as it reached the end of Banbury Road at St Giles. Gilmoss (MTL of Liverpool) sold on twenty-five Leyland Titans, as acquired, to COMS, the majority being X- and Y-registered examples. With its newly converted destination blind box the bus is followed by Midland Red South's Optare Starrider 426 (F846 TLU), which is working the X40 to Birmingham branded in Citylink livery. (Author's collection)

The Go-Ahead Group was a fond user of the Volvo B10B chassis, and later the B10BLE. Plaxton's Verde bodywork was also popular with Oxford Bus, which ran forty-three new single- and dual-door examples. Busy route 52 had been upgraded with the type from Leyland Titans by the time of this 18 February 1998 scene. To dual-door configuration, 637 (P637 FFC) is at the railway station terminus where the area would soon undergo redevelopment.

As Thames Transit developed, larger vehicles were required. By 1994 fourteen Dennis Darts with thirty-nine-seat dual-door Plaxton Pointer bodywork had been delivered. The inaugural route 1 was the recipient with the colour code red still featuring on the destination blinds. Branded as 'Blackbird Flyer' and featuring the character 'Bertie blackbird' who was used in marketing material, 3006 (L715 JUD) heads along Worcester Street in June 1994. (Author's collection)

Further batches were received over the following two years upgrading many of the other city and some rural routes. Each featured distinctive branding and no third party advertising, a Transit Holdings policy. There were two 'Cavalier' brands applied to the route 7 group. As depicted, 'The City Cavalier' covered Barton to Cutteslowe services while the 'Kidlington Cavalier' continued north to that destination. 3036 (M87 WBW) turns onto Cornmarket Street at Carfax on 21 July 1997.

The area of Cutteslowe was served as a terminating loop or diversion off the main Banbury Road, which can be seen behind the bus. COMS 637 (P637 FFC) waits at the first stop on Harbord Road while operating route 2C, part of the unusual '2Z' running card on 5 September 2001. This was a Monday to Friday AM peak hours-only operation between here and the city, to improve headway on the main road.

Numerically the first Volvo B10B, 601 (N601 FJO) waits at Wolvercote cemetery, Banbury Road, on 27 July 2001 depicting the single-door fifty-one-seat layout. Suffix letters were applied to the Kidlington end of the route as an indication of the final destination. The 'Radcliffe Camera' logo forming part of the Oxford fleet name would soon be removed because of copyright issues. The bus is now preserved.

By 2001 six members of the ECW-bodied Leyland Olympian batch still remained for queue-buster duties. Usually appearing only at peak times to offer greater capacity and help maintain frequencies, during the busy summer period some would work all day. Assisting on '2 road' on 23 July 2001 at Queens Lane, 224 (CUD 224Y) heads for Barton. These immaculately kept vehicles were also loaned to other Go-Ahead Group companies as and when required.

Transit Holdings transferred vehicles around its various companies as the need arose or new operations were established. At Carfax in August 1992 working route 3 from Rose Hill was 399 (H790 GTA), a twenty-nine-seat Carlyle-bodied Mercedes-Benz 811D. This dual-purpose vehicle was part of a large batch used by the Group's 'Red Admiral' Portsmouth operation. Fitted with automatic gearboxes they were a significant upgrade for the drivers and passengers compared to the Ford Transits and gave a lively ride. (Author's collection)

Oxfordshire's first low-floor vehicles were Dennis Dart SLF's with Alexander ALX200 bodies launched on 10 February 1998. These twenty-nine vehicles were to a standard Stagecoach Group design with national brand name 'Lo-Liner' and initially used on routes 3, 7 and 7A. Resting at Horspath Road depot with stablemates of similar body design, but with Volvo B6BLE chassis, 826 would work the majority of its life with Stagecoach North-East. (Author's collection)

COMS were not far behind, launching ten vehicles on 1 July 1998 carrying Wright Crusader bodywork paired to the Dennis Dart SLF chassis. The 13 group of routes was the lucky recipient of these dual-door vehicles, which cost the company £850,000, and was the main service between the city and the JR Hospital. The buses and drivers on '13 road' also worked route 6 and seen at Wolvercote terminus on Sunday 12 August 2001 is 410 (R410 FFC). The 6A was the evening and Sunday variant running via Jerico and Walton Street. The bus was one of several Oxford vehicles to transfer to Go West Midlands (Diamond) in 2007.

The first batch of 'Nipper' minibuses had worked the JR Hospital routes, then numbered in the 70 group. MCW and Optare Metroriders replaced the Ford Transits with 775 (G775 WFC) representing the Optare type at St Aldates in June 1994. The driver will use Speedwell Street to turn around before loading on the opposite side of the road for the vehicle's next journey, for which the electronic blind has already been set. (Author's collection)

From late 1994 the Optare Metroriders were repainted into Cityline red livery, with a handful surviving until mid-2000. One such example was caught at Long Hanborough on 18 October 1998 working park and ride duties on behalf of the Oxford Bus Museum. After withdrawal the vehicles were snapped up by other operators, in this case Emsworth & District who returned it to 'Nipper' colours for their fleet.

COMS trialled four battery-powered Optare Metroriders from 1 November 1993. Under contract from Southern Electric the joint venture saw seven drivers work the 'City Circuit' route numbered 5. Each had a range of only 50 miles from full charge and the additional weight meant that only eighteen seats could be fitted. The original contract was for one year but COMS retained it until November 1997. Stagecoach Oxford then worked the route until June 1999 and during this era 801 (L801 HJO) re-charges at the railway station on 18 February 1998. When withdrawn, the buses were to have been used as tour vehicles at UK power stations. However, three went to JMT in Jersey instead, the bus depicted becoming J 30442 numbered E1.

Loading in brilliant sunshine at Magdalen Street on 21 July 1997 is Thames Transit 3042 (M95 WBW). Fifty-five of the type, fitted with dual-doors, were in use at the time with none of the fleet numbers matching their registration marks. Strong branding is applied for 'The Carousel' circular routes 10 and 10A.

With the dawning of the low-floor era the need for a step-entrance demonstrator became obsolete. Owned by Dennis, P452 BPH was a Lance chassis with Northern Counties Paladin bodywork. The company had loaned it to Plaxtons for use by COMS when members of the 'Verde' batch were away for warranty work. Carrying fleet number 699 it approaches Green Road roundabout on 18 February 1998 and overtakes a Stagecoach-owned Oxford Tube coach standing at a well-decorated bus stop pole.

In April 1997 COMS acquired thirteen vehicles with similar bodywork on Volvo B10B chassis from Go-Ahead-owned London General. These were the former London Buses VN class, carrying select 'K-KLL' registrations for route 88 operated by Stockwell Garage. All received full refurbishment and re-registration before entering service. 656 (K130 BUD, K13 KLL) is at Downside Road, Risinghurst, route 22's easterly terminus, on 28 August 2001 with a fresh coat of paint recently applied. The bus would soon be heading cross-city to Brookes University campus at Harcourt Hill.

In September 2003 Brookes Bus was launched for services operated on behalf of the university which were also available to the general public. Stagecoach initially operated the routes, and vehicles were painted in this dedicated livery. 18056 (KX56 VNG) was a Transbus Trident with smart President bodywork, an unusual choice for Stagecoach. During university summer holidays, surplus vehicles were sent to the south-west where they were deployed on routes around Torbay. Photographed at Exeter on 16 September 2009, this vehicle would not be returning to Oxford as COMS had won the Brookes Bus contract on re-tender. 18056 was still in use in 2021 at Cowdenbeath depot. (Raymond Bedford)

Thames Transit's original dual-door Dennis Darts received a refreshed livery in early 1997 as carried on 3004 (L713 JUD) loading at Queen Street on 21 July that year. Stagecoach had just taken over and the Group's familiar stripes would soon appear. 'Bertie Blackbird' would still feature as part of local branding on this 24-hour service. (Author's collection)

MAN products were in favour with Stagecoach when this 28 July 1999 view was taken of Alexander ALX300 bodied MAN 18.220, the first of the original batch new in October 1998. Wearing corporate livery, 'Lo-Liner' became a generic term for the Group's low-floor vehicles. The driving position was also low and 'hail and ride' lettering still featured beside the destination blind. The 'other' well-known university city also had a large batch of this type of vehicle.

COMS were again quick to follow with fifteen full-size low-floor vehicles of the Volvo B10BLE/ Wright Renown combination. These dual-door vehicles were initially used on route 52 to Blackbird Leys with 809 (T809 CBW) pictured loading on Queen Street on 28 July 1999. As part of the city centre code of conduct, engines were switched off when the buses were stationary. The destination blinds were set electronically, and when the ignition was re-engaged the blind would roll up and down one screen – hence the arrangement shown.

ECW-bodied Leyland Olympian 214 (BBW 214Y) of 1982 vintage was seen at Grovelands, Kidlington, on 30 August 2001 whilst working route 2A. Staff of all grades within the company could work these summer queue-buster duties, up to and including the managing director. The bus would stay local and work for Woottens Coaches of Chesham from 2003 and is now part of the Oxford Bus Museum collection.

At George Street, beside the old fire station and Corn Exchange, MAN 932 (S932 CFC) is heading towards Kidlington on 21 September 2001. The 7A was Stagecoach Oxford's version of COMS 2A. The bus had been repainted from the 'gold top' roof and cantrail variation and would soon be renumbered into the 22xxx class.

Waiting for the green light at Magdalen Street beside Oxford Martyrs' Memorial on 10 June 2009 is 22765 (OU58 GKF), a MAN Lion's City with ADL Enviro 300 body. Eleven of these updated vehicles entered service in early 2009 carrying corporate colours and branding to a Group standard. A route map was displayed by the doors and advertising for Megabus can also be seen.

In 2002 COMS moved from Volvo to Mercedes-Benz for single-deck deliveries. Initially five of the elegant Citaro model were used on P&R duties serving the new Water Eaton site. By the time of this 2 June 2008 view forty-eight were in service across the city. The JR Hospital routes were projected to the rail station where 865 (FF57 OXF) is loading. Some journeys also ran to Abingdon as X13. 'City' branding and all-round CCTV cameras feature, as does the abbreviated term for the manufacturer's name, courtesy of a replacement glass cove panel.

395 Cowley Road

Traditional NBC coach types were soon changed by COMS to the more unusual. In 1992 six Dennis Javelins were delivered carrying Plaxton's new Premiere 320 bodywork. The leader of the batch, 50 (K750 UJO), stands at the exit of Cowley Road depot on 18 February 1998 carrying an overall advert for VCS, a destination the coach would have visited many times in its six-year career at Oxford. Headrest covers were still in use and the green livery bears close resemblance to that used some years later on 'Express' branded vehicles.

Nearing retirement, Willowbrook Warrior-bodied Leyland Leopard ABW 310X rests outside 'E garage' on 11 August 2001. At the time, this was one of only three semi-automatic vehicles still in use by the company. New in 1982 as VUD 33X with forty-nine-seat ECW bodywork, a total of six Leopards were re-bodied in 1990 and used on P&R work. After four years all would become driver trainers. A trio of Leyland Lynxes would soon upgrade the training fleet whereupon T4 was sold to Woottens Coaches.

The Willowbrook Warrior styling resembled that of the Leyland Lynx with one of the trio mentioned above acquired from Travel West Midlands where it had performed the same role. C63 HOM was previously TWM 9063 (new as 1063) and extensive re-panelling is underway in the body shop on 8 September 2001. The moulded plastic wheel arches have been replaced and the sign on the wall informs us that health and safety was everyone's responsibility. In 2004 all three followed Leopard T4 to Woottens Coaches where their interiors were restored to as-original condition.

All manner of tasks were carried out on site at Cowley Road. Awaiting the next stage of repaint to its Northern Counties bodywork is Volvo B10B 650 (K124 BUD, K70 KLL) standing near the exit from 'E garage' on 11 August 2001. In late 2005 the batch would move to Bluestar at Southampton.

With no queue busting required on Saturday 8 September 2001, four of the five remaining ECW-bodied Leyland Olympians rest in 'G garage'. Looking spruce, right to left, 214, 220, 221 and 222 would all see service with other operators when withdrawn in 2003.

The old adage 'you wait ages for a bus then four turn up at once' rings true in this view outside Cowley Road garage on 18 February 1998. Roughly ten Ford Transits worth of seats head the procession in the shape of the Alexander RL-bodied Volvo Olympians – then only a few weeks old. At the time Stagecoach had specified this type for its London operations but with analogue blinds. The Hannover blind of 519 is alternating between the ultimate destination and an advert for the Blackbird Flyer (now Bertie-less) Two of COMS' Plaxton Verde-bodied Volvo B10Bs, also with dual-doors, follow. Crew changes could be made at this location.

Around and Out of the County

While looking resplendent in the colour scheme worn when first acquired by COMS, Leyland Titan 975 (A869 SUL) was actually akin to Frankenstein's monster. Having suffered damage to its upper deck while with LT it was sent to MTL for disposal. Whilst there, the complete roof from T146 was used to repair the bus and, just as RT and RM types left Aldenham with different body and chassis combinations, 975 left Liverpool with decks from two different vehicles. Preserved with Woottens Coaches at the time of this picture, taken at Showbus, Duxford, on 16 September 2007, the bus is now owned by the Imperial Bus Diner Co. at Le Pontet, France.

Oxford had seen the Leyland Titan prior to 1993, with South Midland operating six of the type in the late 1980s. Acquired from GMPTE in 1987 they wore the colourful and rather busy paintwork shown on 704 (GNF 10V) which gleams at the Southsea Bus Rally that year. Their lives in Oxfordshire were brief; soon after Thames Transit took over, the batch was sold to Cheltenham & Gloucester. (Author's collection)

COMS were early users of minibuses for specific routes and duties pre-privatisation. New in August 1985, Ford Transit 14 (C114 DJO) was from a batch of seventeen with Carlyle bodywork. It was almost obligatory for operators to give their minibus networks a snazzy name, 'Bustler' in this case. Awaiting its next duty at Bicester depot, the bus would be retained when Transit Holdings took over and later saw life with the Group in Torbay. (Author's collection)

Optare wrote their own chapter of the manufacturers' rule book with some radical designs entering the market. The City Pacer was paired with a VW chassis and certainly threw off the 'bread van' image. It aimed high for orders and newly privatised South Midland took nine in 1986 painted in this blue and silver livery. D230 TBW was numbered 32 and all were withdrawn soon after Transit Holdings acquired the operation. This example found a new home with Lincoln Coaches and is seen at dealers Moseley. Clean socks and polished shoes were the order of the day with the driver perched in full view! (Author's collection)

Complementing Alexander's ALX range the ALX100 was a twenty-nine-seat minibus body available on the Mercedes-Benz Vario chassis. Around 150 were produced with Stagecoach Oxford receiving thirteen. In the then new Stagecoach colours 377 (S377 DFC) works the only journey to Swindon from Witney on Sundays-only route 7. Picking up at 09:48 in the Gloucestershire village of Lechlade on 3 March 2002 the bus would spend the day working between Swindon and Highworth, returning to Witney in the evening. The batch transferred to Kent, this example being renumbered 42377. One still survived as a mobile home in 2021.

After acquiring South Midlands a handful of full-sized vehicles was used by Thames Transit on the Bicester and Woodstock corridors. In 1989 four virtually new Plaxton Derwent-bodied Leyland Tigers arrived from Devon, where they had been acquired with the Burton's of Brixham business. 998 (F281 HOD) has worked from Woodstock and is in the company of vehicles loading for London at the newly refurbished Gloucester Green facility. The bus went on to work for Tillingbourne. (Author's collection)

Keeping the same backdrop the vehicle types had changed in this 21 July 1997 scene. A trio of Plaxton Verde-bodied Dennis Lance were received in 1996 to replace the Leyland Tigers. Of similar appearance to COMS Volvo B10Bs being delivered around the same time, this simple and attractive livery was carried by all three buses. Under Stagecoach ownership this bus became 27901 and transferred to Cumbria. All three would later work for the Birmingham Coach Company's Diamond Bus operation, eventually owned by Go-Ahead Group.

To enhance the single-deck fleet two Dennis Darts were acquired in January 1997 from Gascoigne (East Devon) when still only a few months old. The pair carried unusual UVG bodywork fitted with forty coach seats and wore the previous operator's colours while with Thames Transit, not too dissimilar to their own fleet livery. 428 (N428 FOW) works through Witney in May 1997. The pair departed soon into the Stagecoach era. This example returned south-west to First Western National as 9719 while the other ran for a number of operators across the UK. (Author's collection)

February 1998 saw the arrival of nine handsome Northern Counties Paladins. Around this time, Stagecoach allocated the type to several of its fleets alongside the more common Alexander-PS. Late model Volvo B10M chassis powered the buses which were delivered to Oxford at the same time as some low-floor Dennis Darts. The batch settled on the Bicester routes with 905 viewed at Magdalen Street passing Debenhams, then under refurbishment. The yellow 'Bus Points' vinyl in the windscreen advertised a scheme which was similar to supermarket loyalty cards. Later numbered 20005 the bus saw further use with Stagecoach South's Aldershot depot. (Author's collection)

The 'S Series' route network was launched by Stagecoach Oxford in 2009 and upgraded the operator's major interurban corridors. Strong branding, ticket deals, high-frequency and 24-hour service were fundamentals of the 'Superior Series'. On 10 June 2009 ADL Trident 18395 (KX55 TLO) was on George Street running the route formerly numbered 100. The rolling stock would soon be upgraded with this vehicle now employed within the Group's south-west division.

The busy Oxford to Bicester corridor became the S5 in 2009. It was previously the 27 group of routes with lettered suffixes serving multiple destinations around the market town. Early 2008 saw Stagecoach trial twenty-five Scania N230UD chassis in Oxford and Manchester. Carrying the more familiar ADL Enviro 400 bodywork, thirteen were used on the Bicester route. 15442 (KX08 KZN) was resting between trips on 12 February 2011 at the rather cramped and basic Bure Place bus station. Stagecoach clearly liked the Scania product, going on to order nearly a thousand.

The success of the 'S Series' upgrades saw all converted to 'gold' status within a short space of time. The S1 and S2 were again first in line and Scania 15535 (VX59 JCZ), diverted from Cheltenham & Gloucester, shows the discreet route branding carried. On 11 July 2010 it was away from home being one of over 250 Stagecoach buses working P&R routes to Silverstone for the annual Formula 1 race. This is the Hinton Airfield site near Brackley.

On loan to Stagecoach Oxford in 2011 was this smart Alexander-Dennis Enviro 400 demonstrator. Numbered 80015 for its stay, it slotted in well to the 'S Series' routes having a full tick-list of optional features fitted to its new-style body. Oxford-bound on 12 February 2011, the eager group of waiting passengers will shortly agree with the side promotional advert! COMS also tried out this vehicle which was eventually sold to Mc Gill's of Barrhead.

The former London Buses VN class were regulars on the 4-road services. Suffix letters only applied to westbound destinations all running the same way from the city to Rose Hill, with frequencies of up to every seven minutes. At Queen Street on 18 February 1998, 653 (K127 BUD, K10 KLL) carrying Cityline branding and 'dreaming spires' logo, had arrived from Elms Rise.

At The Oval, Rose Hill, COMS 642 (P642 FFC) waits to leave the turning circle for the city and Dean Court working '4H card' on 17 September 2001. One of the dual-door Plaxton Verde batch, it waits in company with two locally built Rover cars. Now owned by BMW for production of the new Mini, the factory has always been a draw for labour affecting recruitment by the city's bus operators.

Soon after Stagecoach acquired Thames Transit the Group's familiar livery began to appear. Wearing stripes, 3026 (M75 VJO) works the Abingdon Express on 18 February 1998 while passing stablemate 3058 (N58 KBW) in a previous generic unbranded livery. A member of the M-registered Dennis Dart batch is now preserved. Carfax Tower, seen beside the pair, had been managed by Tappins Coaches' sightseeing division on behalf of Oxford City Council.

COMS' Abingdon express is represented here on 21 July 1997 by Volvo B10B 627 (N415 NRG) laying over at Bonn Square while making the loop back to St Aldates. One of four diverted from Go-North East in 1995 to upgrade the fleet, their slight livery differences made them easy to spot. Competition was reflected in the twenty-minute frequency of the route with a weekly ticket costing £8. The bus was one of seven transferred to High Wycombe in 1999.

Extra capacity was provided on this popular route when ex-P&R Dennis Trident 120 (T120 DBW) was given freedom to leave the city boundary repainted red with dedicated route branding. Due to mileage accumulation the 'red' Trident would rotate with other vehicles after a period of time. The mint green interior gives away the P&R heritage as the bus waits to work the 17:35 from Oxford rail station on 28 July 2001.

A slower journey to Abingdon was on offer by COMS on routes 4 via Cumnor or 35/A via Kennington with, at that time, some journeys continuing to Didcot. Interesting traction on 21 July 1997 was Leyland Titan 956 (KYV 519X) at Queen Street. The Wayfarer 3 ticket machine and magnetic card validator will be noted, along with off-side advertising for Freedom tickets. The Titan era ended soon afterwards with all examples being sold for further service. The subject of the picture was re-registered WAZ 8276 and went with several others to Kimes of Folkingham.

The long-established link between Oxford and Aylesbury, once numbered 82, ran via Thame and Haddenham. The MAP scheme changed them to 280/1/2 and during NBC times even linked them to the Kidlington corridor. In 1990 six Leyland Olympians with smart Alexander AL bodies were delivered. They featured Gardner engines, BET-style windscreens and dual doors, and were regular performers on the Aylesbury and Reading routes. Seen when new and carrying a good load the last of the batch waits to turn onto Cornmarket Street, surrounded by period cars. Converted to single door and transferred to High Wycombe in 1995, the bus would remain with that depot's successor, Arriva, clocking up nearly twenty years service. Today the 280 remains, its route almost unaltered since this view was taken. (Author's collection)

The South Midland division had a long association with Aylesbury, garaging vehicles there until 1987, and for a short time Thames Transit competed on the 280 using minibuses. COMS' association would end in July 1995 with this scene, at the Market Square, taken a few weeks before on 11 May. Under Go-Ahead ownership a brand refresh took place in late 1994 with Cityline red vehicles running city and interurban routes. The driver wears the appropriate matching red tie and epaulettes. Ford of Althorne acquired the bus in 2003. (Author's collection)

Roughly halfway between Oxford and Aylesbury lies the historic market town of Thame. Luton & District ran services 260/1 and 280 here from Aylesbury. From 23 July 1995 L&D acquired the whole route through to Oxford, COMS withdrawing completely by November to concentrate on their city network. Early production ECW-bodied Leyland Olympian 612 (ARP 612X) is about to enjoy the extension beyond Thame in this June 1996 scene. All nine of the batch were long-term residents at Aylesbury and later received The Shires blue and yellow livery. (Author's collection)

By now branded for Arriva The Shires, Leyland Olympian G234 VWL returned to old territory when working from Aylesbury depot. Now numbered 5834 the bus had transferred from High Wycombe. Having worked through numerous villages to reach Thame High Street on 2 June 2008, the route would be retraced on its return.

Park & Ride

In 1973 the UK's first P&R service was pioneered in Oxford. Initially, car parks were located to the north, south and west of the city offering free parking, with buses running every thirty minutes with fares of 40p return during the peak and 30p off-peak. A batch of Daimler Fleetlines with MCW bodies was acquired from London Transport with most wearing an overall white livery with local advertising. However 998 (MLH 371L) wore NBC poppy red and in this view shows the adapted destination blind and Timtronic ticket machine. It is picking up a good load at Magdalen Street and will head south to Redbridge car park, the low railway station bridge limiting 9xx series vehicles to the north–south route. (Author's collection)

In 1988 COMS received five Alexander RL-bodied Leyland Olympians specifically for P&R duties. Delivered in overall white with painted destination boxes, local advertising featured on each vehicle between decks. By the time of this 26 July 1989 scene at St Aldates, Thames Transit were operating their north to south P&R route 9, as evidenced by the Ford Transit minibus behind. Two very different styles of product were therefore on offer to those heading back to their cars. (Author's collection)

999 was something unique – an early prototype Leyland B45 bodied by Alexander for demonstration in Singapore. Exhibited at the 1980 Commercial Motor Show as a ninety-seven-seater with 'tropical' windows, the bus was registered SBS 5396B for its use in the Far East. Arriving at Oxford in 1987 it received 'local' UK registration PWL 999W, was re-glazed, re-seated to eighty-four and received an ECW-style front end. Captured in July 1992 on its regular P&R duties, it is has just passed the Oxford Martyrs' Memorial heading along St Giles. Plain white livery features again as does a chasing Thames Transit vehicle on similar work. After a spell at High Wycombe the Olympian entered preservation. (Author's collection)

Thames Transit's route 9 received a 'touch of class' in 1994 with the arrival of new chauffer 'Gloria Glide'. Six Mellor-bodied Iveco 59.12s received this livery, which featured contravison over the windows in the form of a limousine. Seeking out custom at Pear Tree car park in August 1994 is 2088 (L948 EOD), which featured dual doors. Both operators' bus stop flags and publicity feature on the lamp post as does a car park-facing CCTV camera. (Author's collection)

Under Go-Ahead from October 1994 P&R services were spruced up with the introduction of this green, white and blue livery. Looking much more attractive, 228 (E228 CFC) was still plying its trade on P&R routes complete with retro-fitted destination blind. Two years after this 21 July 1997 view the bus moved, with others of the batch, to Wycombe Bus and ended its days with Arriva at Southend.

Joining the E-registered Olympians and 999 in the P&R fleet were a handful of Leyland Titans and ECW-bodied Leyland Olympians. Some received an interior refurbishment and the destination blinds were utilised more effectively. 216 (BBW 216Y) was seen at St Aldates on 29 June 1998 displaying promotional material along with the colour code and symbol for Redbridge car park.

On Tuesday June 1999 COMS introduced twenty low-floor Dennis Tridents with Alexander ALX400 bodywork. The £2.7 million investment by the company was specifically aimed at the P&R routes and the easy-access vehicles wore the livery introduced in 1994. Numerically the first, 101 (T101 DBW) works route 300 on the 'A-card' at Redbridge car park on 20 August 2001.

A long-term loan to COMS from Alexander, while warranty work took place, was Dennis Trident V929 VMS. Wearing this attractive livery when viewed at Pear Tree car park on 25 August 2001, it stayed long enough to receive the updated P&R livery also captured in model form by Corgi. The vehicle later saw use with Kimes of Folkingham.

A decade later, in 2011, the next generation of vehicle and propulsion arrived for P&R routes. Eighteen Alexander Dennis Enviro 400H diesel electric hybrids were delivered in an updated livery showing the five car park sites by then available. Looking pristine in this July 2011 view, 312 (HW11 OXF) demonstrates the good loads carried on these services as it leaves the bus lane to enter the Redbridge car park stop. The batch lasted far longer than the four battery-powered Metroriders of 1993. This example still currently works for COMS. (Author's collection)

As we have seen before, Oxford's two main operators are never far behind each other with new types being launched. In 2010 Stagecoach Oxford had introduced twenty-six similar Alexander Dennis Enviro 400Hs in corporate style. Last of the batch, 12026 (OU10 GFZ), breezes along a deserted Banbury Road on 12 February 2011. The livery was a pleasing variant which had previously been used on the Group's services in the Lake District. The newest P&R site, Water Eaton, opened in 2002 and can be seen behind the bus. The grain silo has since been demolished and the area now houses Oxford Parkway railway station.

Coaching and Citylinking

In 1984/5 COMS received eight MCW Metroliners in two batches for Citylink duties. These sixty-six-seaters principally worked route 190 to London Victoria but could also be seen on the airport services. Exemplifying the latter is 904 (B904 XJO) departing Heathrow Central bus station in July 1985. At the time, MCW sought a share of the double-deck coach market but only 172 examples were built. Withdrawn in 1992 the coach ended its days, along with several others of the type, as an open-top sightseeing bus in London. (Author's collection)

Seven years would pass before the Oxford to London corridor would see double-deck coaches again. Operating for Thames Transit's successor, these were Jonckheere Monaco-bodied MAN 24.350s. Following an amazing launch event at Gloucester Green on 29 March 1999, the twenty-seven wheelchair-accessible coaches were phased onto the Oxford Tube over a period of five months. They replaced an assortment of single-deck coaches of mainly Thames Transit origin. Their livery was a nice take on the stripes used by the Stagecoach Group at the time with 45 (T45 BBW) heading a line-up at Grosvenor Gardens on 14 April 2002. A considerable mileage would have already been clocked up. Note the use of the registered trademark symbol after the fleet name.

Plaxton is paramount in this scene at Victoria coach station 'Departures' on 23 April 1993. COMS 141, a DAF with low driving position, and Dennis Javelin 50 await return to Oxford. Running alongside more traditional NBC-era Leyland Tigers, Volvo products would eventually rule supreme. COMS used the main VCS site right up until the last day of operation, 4 January 2020.

A low-key private hire identity was carried on a handful of COMS coaches in the 1980s/early 1990s. 109 (EBW 109Y) was one of a batch of ten Duple Dominant IV Express-bodied Leyland Tigers new in 1983 – the last for the company with this body styling. Operating a more routine duty on route 190 at Buckingham Palace Road, the coach would later receive standard Citylink 'Venetian blind' livery. Five of the batch saw use in High Wycombe before withdrawal. (Author's collection)

A number of coaches were inherited with the purchase of the South Midland operation, some utilised on 'The Tube'. Leyland Tiger 11 (LSV 670, C129 KJO) was previously numbered 129 and was travelling up New Road on 26 July 1989. Original-style lettering has been applied to the overall white livery and the name 'Queens College' was also carried. (Author's collection)

As early as 1990 new coaches were received for the route, which was officially numbered 100. The chassis of choice was the Volvo B10M with some exotic bodywork fitted. 22 (H916 FTT) was one of five registered new in Exeter in 1991, and carried Ikarus 'Blue Danube' bodywork. Some similar second-hand examples were also added to the fleet. The original London terminus was at Marble Arch but had moved to Grosvenor Gardens, Victoria, by the time of this 23 April 1993 view.

Following on from the large batches of Ford Transits were Mercedes-Benz 709Ds carrying Reeve Burgess bodywork. The first twenty-five had dual-purpose seating and some were painted into Oxford Tube livery for routes considered to be 'feeder' services. Fellow vehicles 322 and 323 meet at Bonn Square on 26 July 1989, advertising the London operation. (Author's collection)

COMS and Thames Transit competed relatively peacefully in both bus and coach operations. However, from time to time some 'cage rattling' took place. In 1996, TT returned to 1987 pricing with their £2.97 day return fare. COMS applied this to the Citylink service, by then numbered X90, as advertised on the front of 162 (UJI 1762, H960 DRJ). The Plaxton Paramount-bodied Volvo B10M was one of five acquired from Shearings in 1995 and is departing VCS for the 61-mile return journey home which would take around ninety minutes. (Author's collection)

Jonckheere-bodied coaches followed those of Ikarus on the Oxford Tube. By the time of this 21 July 1997 view the service was running twenty-four hours a day and celebrating its tenth birthday. Vehicles received this gold and red livery variation and Volvo B10M L212 GJO, numbered 5, waits on George Street for space to become available in Gloucester Green, a frequent occurrence. It is carrying the name and crest of Magdalen College which would later be removed following a rights-of-use issue. The coach later saw service locally with Motts Travel of Aylesbury.

After five years the whole fleet of twenty-seven Jonckheere Monacos were replaced, through Dawson Rentals, with twenty-five Neoplan Skyliners. Eighty-six seats were on offer and we see another variation of the corporate livery in use at the time. Prior to their entry into service trials were conducted at night for manoeuvrability on the route. At Gloucester Green, Bay 1 has been removed to create additional space. On 2 June 2008, 50115 (KP04 GKF) shows one of several rear adverts promoting the route. Stagecoach had used this type of coach on its pioneering Scotland to London services in the early 1980s.

Complete fleet replacement would occur again in 2009 and see another body and chassis combination introduced. Twenty-six Van Hool Astromega eighty-seven-seaters took to the road wearing a livery to the same style as their predecessors. 50206 (OU09 FMY) was at Buckingham Palace Road, now the terminal point, on 5 August 2009 when brand new. The type would also be introduced on Megabus workings in both the UK and North America.

The familiar blue, white and yellow livery seen on the X90 was changed in 2004. Offering a very different package to its competitor, 'Espress' was sold on maximum legroom and high-spec fittings such as DVD players, power points and later, Wi-Fi. For this civilised café-culture inspired look seven Irizar Century-bodied Scania K114EBs were received and carried on the tradition of select registration marks. P1 OXF was originally numbered 62 but was changed to 40 by the time of this 17 August 2011 angle taken at Marble Arch. The association with Brookes University is conveyed by the lettering on the door. (Author's collection)

The last vehicles delivered under Grandforce Ltd (the company name of the original management buyout team) ownership were six Volvo B10Ms carrying Plaxton Premiere 350 bodies. Received in December 1993 for use on airport routes they would later follow the time-honoured migration to the London service. Bearing suffix letters previously carried on two batches of Bristol VRs 151 (L151 HUD) turns from Thames Street into St Aldates heading for Heathrow in June 1994. Further service was seen with Worths of Enstone and Confidence of Leicester. (Author's collection)

The Plaxton Excalibur was the popular choice for the company between 1998 and 2001. The first member of the final batch of six, 23 (Y23 OXF) was exhibited when new at Duxford Showbus Rally on 23 September 2001. Body styling details can be compared to the previous picture of the main Plaxton products on offer at the time, as can the updated livery. Soon to be branded 'Airline', new deliveries would move away from the Volvo chassis. The coach would go on to serve with De Courcey of Coventry.

Nineteen Leyland Leopards with Duple Dominant II bodies were received between 1977 and 1979. Having worked the Oxford to London route when new, 7 (PJO 7T) joined South Midland with the 1983 split. It is carefully negotiating its exit from VCS in an era when suitcases were carried by hand. Taking a route along the Thames Valley, the coach would serve Oxford before completing its journey at Wantage where, at the time, it and fourteen other vehicles were based in Grove Street garage. (Author's collection)

Green Line kept a presence on the Oxford to London corridor until July 1996 when the route was curtailed (except on Sundays) at High Wycombe. Numbered into the Oxford South Midland series this was a meandering route along the A40. In years past a number of peak-time variations saw journeys serve villages along the route. Newly repainted into the standard Green Line scheme was Luton & District's TPL92 (B292 KPF), a Plaxton Paramount 3200-bodied Leyland Tiger based at High Wycombe depot. Pictured on Worcester Street in June 1994, the coach has just set off from Gloucester Green on the 15:00 route 291 departure, a variant running direct from Loudwater to Marble Arch. This would position it in time for a commuter run back to High Wycombe. Eight Leyland Tigers were allocated to that town at the time, this example becoming 4012 upon formation of The Shires. (Author's collection)

Sightseeing with Open-toppers

Another long-serving Amersham and High Wycombe vehicle, new to London Country as AN236, was Roe-bodied Leyland Atlantean JPE 236V. Later numbered 5040 with The Shires it was one of the last of its type in use at Wycombe and was withdrawn in 1998, after which it was converted to open top. Guide Friday operated eight vehicles in Oxford, at the time maintained and housed at Cowley Road. COMS fleet numbers were unofficially applied for administrative purposes. Amidst historic architecture on Broad Street, the driver welcomes aboard some much-needed custom on 4 September 2001.

Also offering a tour of Oxford's sights was Lothian-owned The Oxford Classic Tour. It was operated on their behalf from April 1990 by Tappins Coaches using five Alexander-bodied Leyland AN68s. The oldest of these Scottish vehicles was BFS 14L, named *The Oxford Student*, which was heading along Worcester Street in June 1994. The places it would visit, the languages available and the prices charged are clearly displayed on the side of the bus. Leyland Olympians would replace the Atlanteans. (Author's collection)

Guide Friday became part of City Sightseeing and their bright livery was soon applied to the Oxford allocation. Tappins Coaches took care of the fleet which by 2008 was modernised with four former Dublin Bus Alexander RH-bodied Leyland Olympians. 53 (MUI 7853, 90-D-1012) awaits its next tour circuit at the railway station terminus on 2 June 2008. COMS would take over the service on behalf of City Sightseeing from 2017.

South Midland offered an open-top service to Blenheim Palace and Woodstock, as well as a city tour route which featured four ex-LT DMS-class vehicles. At Bicester's London Road depot in 1987 OT2 (GHV 121N) is about to head off for another day's work. Acquired from Ensign Bus in 1985, where it was numbered DMO1121, this type was to prove popular on such duties. Thames Transit and even Stagecoach Oxford kept an open-top service running for several summer seasons. (Author's collection)

Coach Operators and Independents

The DMS-class Daimler Fleetlines fell out of favour with LT very early in their careers. New homes were quickly found with operators across the UK and overseas through dealers Ensign Bus. Coaches and buses have been run by the Holder family from the village of Charlton-on-Otmoor since the 1950s. Acquired in 1980 for routes between Bicester and Oxford, Daimler Fleetline MLH 402L shows Ensign's early centre-door conversion style. Complete with Setright ticket machine, it looks immaculate while attending the annual Showbus rally in the company of a similar vehicle, which still hangs on with LT. (Author's collection)

Another coach firm still going strong today is Motts Travel of Aylesbury. In 1991 contract gains saw the establishment of a bus division named 'Yellow Bus' which rapidly expanded to run daily routes, both tendered and commercial, into most of the company's neighbouring counties. This 1994 view of the previous premises in Stoke Mandeville shows the mix of vehicles used on such services. The main double-deck type was the MCW Metrobus, both Mk 1 and Mk 2 designs depicted here. Former South Yorkshire PTE JHE 141W has worked from Oxford on route 280 while ex-London Buses CUB 540Y, new to West Yorkshire PTE, has performed a Herts. CC school contract. Two Willowbrook 003-bodied vehicles are also in view as is part of another ex-DMS-class Daimler on the back row. The Yellow Bus division was taken over by The Shires in July 1995. (Author's collection)

Joining the transport scene in 1998, initially on routes in south Oxfordshire, was Wallingford-based Thames Travel. Numerous contracts followed many acquired with the closure of Tillingbourne and Chiltern Queens. Loading at St Aldates for Henley on 18 September 2001 is Plaxton Beaver-bodied Mercedes-Benz Vario V390 SVV, new in 1999 and one of several of the type in use. The company was sold to the Go-Ahead Group in May 2011.

Tappins Coaches was established at the beginning of the twentieth century with three generations of the family running the operation from their Didcot base. From the 1980s many large supermarket chains were moving stores to out-of-town locations. Tesco provided free shopper buses to a number of sites including its Abingdon store. Contractors provided vehicles in Tesco livery, as shown on former South Wales Transport Leyland National LWN 713L. Having a day off from the weekly shop in October 1986 the bus was exhibited at the Woburn Abbey Showbus rally. (Author's collection)

More typical of Tappins' vehicles was H261 GRY, a Plaxton Paramount 3500-bodied Volvo B10M wearing their bold, distinctive livery and new in April 1991. In 2007 Heyfordian and Weavaway acquired most of Tappins' operations. (Author's collection)

RH Transport of Witney built up a sizeable mixed fleet during the 2000s, principally engaged on contracts and tendered work, until the company suddenly closed its doors in October 2012. During happier times, on 28 September 2008, 601 (F112 OMJ) was representing the company at the annual Showbus rally in Duxford. This Alexander PS-type bodied Scania N113 CRB was new to London Buses in 1989, numbered SA1, and operated alongside contemporary vehicles with a view to finding a new 'standard' single-deck bus for use in the capital.

Swanbrook Coaches of Cheltenham were good customers for COMS, buying many of their used vehicles. Arriving in 2000 was Plaxton Paramount 3500-bodied Volvo B10M UJI 1762, H960 DRJ new to Shearings. Regularly running back to its former home on route 53 from Cheltenham and Gloucester, for which branding was displayed on the side windows, this view is on Magdalen Street East, Oxford, on Sunday 12 August 2001.

Worth's of Enstone also purchased a number of vehicles from COMS. Smartly turned-out Volvo B10M L151 HUD stands on Broad Street on 4 September 2001, diverted from its normal line of route due to the St Giles Street Fair. The coach had been entered in the Brighton Coach Rally that year and would go on to work for Confidence of Leicester.

COMS' twenty-four Leyland Olympians with dual-door ECW bodywork were withdrawn between 1999 and 2003. Their careers at Oxford were varied as were the operators who bought them for further use. New in October 1982, BBW 216Y was acquired by Worth's in June 1999. Its paintwork shines when on display at the Showbus rally in Duxford on 26 September that year.

Bringing a touch of luxury to Worth's long-standing route 69 between Oxford and Chipping Norton is Mercedes-Benz Citaro BU53 ZWZ. Would the manufacturer have approved of Worth's amusing strap line 'For a Rattling Good Ride' displayed on the glass cove panel above the rear wheel? Caught at Chipping Norton on 8 March 2010, it was to be only a matter of weeks before the company ended stage carriage operation on 29 May. The bus then headed south-west to Western Greyhound, but its career was cut short in 2013 after being destroyed in the Summercourt depot fire.

Family-run Grayline operates from Bicester with buses working tendered routes while coaches can be found on tours and hires around the UK and Europe-wide. With no loyalty to any particular chassis or body manufacturer some interesting vehicles have appeared in the fleet such as 947 CBK (G442 WFC), purchased new in 1990. A MAN with Caetano Algarve thirty-one-seat body, it was nearing withdrawal in this early 1996 view. In 2015 the company's Station Approach depot returned to being a railway station, Bicester Village, and new premises are now occupied just outside the town. (Author's collection)

Varsity Links (Oxford to Cambridge)

Routes 131 and 132 linked Oxford with Bedford and were jointly operated by COMS (later South Midland) and United Counties. With the Timtronic ticket machine working overtime, former Potteries Duple-bodied Leyland Leopard 51 (URF 51S) takes an impressive load at Gloucester Green in April 1986. Would a duplicate be required? (Rob Edworthy/Author's collection)

By the time of this 24 August 2004 view the route, now numbered 32, had been substantially cut to run only between Milton Keynes and Buckingham. This council-tendered service, which Jeffs of Helmdon operated for many years, once ran a meandering path to Oxford. Former COMS Marshall-bodied Dennis Dart M505 VJO retains its centre doors and previous owner's livery while laying over at Milton Keynes's Central bus station which is now a (bus-less) Grade II listed building. For a short while the bus had been numbered T5 at Oxford for use as a driver trainer.

Premier Travel of Cambridge had a long-standing service running from Oxford to its home city across Bucks and Herts. Its successor, Cambridge Coach Services, developed a network of routes in the 1990s mainly featuring airports. The 75 commenced in May 1992, initially with four daily return journeys on roughly a two-hourly headway. However, because of the company's professional service and excellent publicity material within two years demand had seen this increase to nine journeys per day. Departing High Wycombe's Newlands bus station is route-branded Plaxton Paramount 3500-bodied Volvo B10M 398 (G98 RGG), new to Parks of Hamilton and carrying the name Downing (a Cambridge University College). National Express would eventually operate and re-shape the service. (Author's collection)

25 September 1995 saw the introduction of Stagecoach United Counties service X5. The simple branding indicates the route taken to link the two cities and six former Wallace Arnold Plaxton Premiere 320-bodied Volvo B10Ms were initially used. Launched with an hourly frequency, two coaches were each allocated to Bedford, Huntingdon and Northampton depots. The Stagecoach Express name was carried by a number of other subsidiary companies at the time. Northampton depot also ran timetabled positioning journeys and their 146 (83 CBD, K758 FYG) rests at Greyfriars bus station on 8 March 1999. Former Oxford Tube coaches would soon replace these vehicles on the route.

The Stagecoach Group's involvement with National Express contracts had decreased significantly by 2004. Coaches used on that work were cascaded to other duties with Bedford depot, now the sole provider, receiving several for the X5. A new livery and branding was introduced but vehicle interiors were not refurbished. At Bure Place in Bicester on 11 June 2008 former Perth-based Volvo B10M 52382 (P622 ESO) carries Plaxton Expressliner 2 bodywork. A fleet of brand-new coaches would soon raise the profile of this route.

Prior to the ordering of the new Volvo B9s for the service, a redundant Bedford-based Volvo Olympian was painted in this special livery and received interior modifications, which included a bicycle rack. This was to canvas public opinion on having double-deckers for the route, but would passengers be happy with a batch of refurbished Volvo Olympians or would they expect something more salubrious?! Leaflets and comment cards were available on-bus to post to Bedford depot or you could express your opinion over the or email the management team. Departing Gloucester Green on 6 June 2008 is 16209 (R34 TAC), which previously carried identities R703 DNH, 83 CBD, R559 DNH and WLT 528.

Into Northamptonshire

The Stagecoach Group's standard double-decker was for many years the Alexander RL-bodied Volvo Olympian. A long-standing Northampton-based example was 16696 (R696 DNH), which shows signs of wintry road conditions while departing Oxford railway station on one of four X6 return journeys. At the time the depot was one of the last to still have vehicles wearing the striped livery. The route was previously numbered X38 and X61, the latter running through to Leicester and Nottingham. The bus remained at Northampton until 2015. (Nigel Wheeler)

The Northampton to Oxford route was renumbered in September 2007 to X88 and co-ordinated with route 88. Five return journeys ran the full length of the 'Gold Star' branded route which should not be confused with the premium product on offer. In order to compete with First on town services, seven Optare Solos were delivered to Northampton in 2004 – two of which later had digital tachographs fitted for their use on the Oxford route. 47126 (KN54 XYU) arrives at Northampton's cavernous Greyfriars bus station, illustrating the smart branding and internal poster holders. The route would be curtailed at Brackley in 2009 with Walters Limousines taking a contracted X88 from that town to Oxford. (Nigel Wheeler)

Cumberland received a batch of Alexander PS-bodied Volvo B10Ms in 1992, with Stagecoach going on to receive nearly 500 examples by 1998 when MAN chassis took over for the low-floor era. The stock was shuffled around constituent companies in the ensuing years as operations dictated. United Counties didn't receive any from new but second-hand examples were received from Midland Red South and Manchester from 2004. Northampton was allocated nine, including 20202 (M202 LHP), formerly of Rugby depot. Once carrying traditional Midland Red livery, by 8 July 2007 it wore corporate colours when viewed at Silverstone village. This was Formula One weekend and a shuttle service was being operated to and from Northampton railway station. The bus is now in preservation.

Midland Red South received twenty-eight Alexander PS-bodied Volvo B10Ms, the final deliveries being alongside low-floor vehicles. Under Stagecoach's South Midland division transfers took place with 20228 (R228 CRW) moving to Oxford. The type mainly worked rural and interurban services and in June 2005 the bus is laying-over at Oxford railway station. (Author's collection)

Jeffs Coaches, founded by Jack Jeffs in 1958, expanded operations by acquiring a number of small local firms, giving them depots in Northamptonshire, Oxfordshire and Buckinghamshire. From Greens Norton depot, which was previously owned by Basfords Coaches, came VKX 510 (formerly XNV 145Y), a Jonckheere Bermuda-bodied Volvo B10M that was exhibited at the 1981 Commercial Motor Show. Jeffs ran numerous examples of the type, owing to an association with the UK distributor whose offices were in Northampton. Having dropped off its party in Ely on 12 April 2002 the coach rests beside a vehicle seventeen years its junior. The registration plate was later owned by Worth's, who acquired it on a different vehicle purchased from Jeffs.

At Witney depot we see Plaxton Supreme III-bodied Leyland Leopard 647 PJO, soon to head off on a college contract. New in 1976 as SGN 331R, the vehicle was acquired in 1987 from local firm Percivals. (Author's collection)

After taking Jonckheere products from the early 1980s, the following decade saw orders switch to Salvador Caetano. Most were coupled to the Volvo B10M, N789 SJU being one of a pair delivered in May 1996 featuring the taller Algarve II bodywork. Passing Victoria Palace Theatre, Jeffs had an extensive tour and excursion programme as well as undertaking private hire, London being a big draw for both activities. (Colin Lloyd/Author's collection)

Once employed on Citylink 190 work YFC 17V, a Leyland Leopard with Duple Dominant II Express body, also served with South Midland painted maroon and cream. Jeffs acquired it in 1990 with the business of Windrush Valley in Witney, whose local phone number is displayed as a destination. Moves between depots were common; a unified livery existed but different fleet names were often used as we have seen. This 10 March 2002 view is at Helmdon depot.

Also acquired from COMS were four Jonckheere Deauville-bodied Volvo B10Ms new to Parks of Hamilton. M630 FNS was pressed into service immediately after arriving and is seen in its former owner's livery. It would soon be repainted and re-registered XWG254. After Jeffs closed the coach was sold to Cannon BBT in the north-west and up-seated to carry seventy passengers.

Jeffs' head office from 1959 was at Helmdon, in rural Northamptonshire, at the old Stratford-upon-Avon and Midland Junction railway station which closed in 1951. Some of the old buildings remained, as can be seen behind freshly repainted 112 AXN, formerly COMS 42 (M628 FNS), which had yet to enter service in this 6 May 2002 view. Automatic transmission was fitted, which was a treat for drivers of a largely manual gearbox fleet.

Former COMS double-deckers also featured in the fleet for schools and contract work, although they sometimes ventured onto private hires should the capacity be required. Ex-South Midland Bristol VR with low-height ECW bodywork CJO 466R carries subsidiary Paynes of Buckingham's fleet name under the windscreen, although by then it was based at the former Windrush premises at Witney. Some unusual ex-Northampton Transport Bristol VRs were also operated. (Author's collection)

In 2000 the Bristol VRs were replaced by Leyland Olympians obtained from a couple of sources. Facing in the railway's 'down' direction beside the old trackbed on 14 April 2000 are Roe-bodied TPD 118X and ECW-bodied WWL 210X, both coming from COMS. The former had been used at High Wycombe and was new to London Country as LR18; the latter was new to Oxford. 210 would be written-off after an accident while the other bus can still be hired today in its non-PSV role as a promotional roadshow vehicle.

In 2004 Jeffs was sold to the Bowen Group of Tamworth who already owned nearby local coach firm Yorks Travel of Cogenhoe. The Group's livery is carried on Van Hool-bodied Volvo B10M 89 (387 TYD, E263 OMT) acquired from Travellers of Hounslow in 1994. Members of the fleet were named after battleships, HMS *Dreadnaught* in this case. Yorks lettering still featured on the front in this view on St Gregory's Road, Northampton, on 17 March 1998. The company closed with the collapse of the Bowen Group in October 2012, their depot now used by Chalfont Coaches for National Express contracts.

Midland Red South Territory

Cherished plates featured on the majority of Heyfordian Travel's fleet, who had depots at Bicester, Witney and High Wycombe. Body and chassis combinations were varied, with this Jonckheere Jubilee P50-bodied Scania K112 being new to the company in 1985. Over the years, identities 9769 UK, 1264 LG and B157 YBW were carried, with the vehicle going on to receive 9682 FH after this view was taken. (Author's collection)

Heyfordian also ran a number of tendered bus routes with a substantial fleet built up by the late 2000s. New in May 2009 for use on Banbury town services was twenty-eight-seat Plaxton Primo KX09 CKC, carrying the livery applied to the bus fleet when seen in the town centre on 8 March 2010. The bus went on to work for WMSNT Enterprise in the Wolverhampton area.

Banbury's principal operator was Midland Red South, the company still serving the town as part of the Stagecoach Group. The Leyland National featured in all corners of Midland Red territory with many examples retained in the south division into the Stagecoach era. Under Western Travel ownership a large number were repowered with DAF engines and received interior refurbishment. 708 (TOF 708S) displays its new badge as it departs Banbury bus station, which was also under refurbishment, for Chipping Norton. The route still carries this number today. (Author's collection)

Coded 'BY', Midland Red opened a garage on Canal Street in October 1919, with extensions made to the side and rear of the original building as services developed. Thirty-two vehicles were allocated here in September 1993 and the doors were still red in this 14 July 1997 scene. Alexander AM-bodied Mercedes-Benz 709D 304 (J304 THP) was one of a pair bought under Western Travel ownership but very much to a Stagecoach standard.

A handful of double-deckers were used at Banbury with their schedules centred on school and college contracts. The Bristol VR was the common type, all being acquired from a variety of sources. This pair transferred through the Stagecoach Group in 1994 and were still wearing their former owners' colours when seen at Banbury depot on 14 July 1997. Resting tightly beside the wall 932 (CBV 16S) came from Ribble while dual-door 927 (NHU 671R) joined from Cheltenham & Gloucester.

Training vehicles and open-toppers were generally the more unusual time-expired vehicles. Often a challenge to master, the phrase 'if you can drive this you can drive anything' was commonly heard. Banbury's T5 (MCS 139W) was a Bedford YLQ with Duple Dominant II body new to Western Scottish in 1981 numbered E573, and acquired from Arran Coaches. Tuition complete, it was being parked up for the night on 14 July 1997.

Midland Red South ran a substantial fleet of minibuses spread across all depots. LDV Sherpa, Iveco and Mercedes-Benz types were bought new, supplemented with some acquired examples. From Beaton of Blantyre in 1992 came this 'stretched' Alexander AM-bodied Mercedes-Benz 811D. Numbered 419 and with thirty-three 'DP' seats, on 14 July 1997 the vehicle had been working routes serving the established Bretch Hill area of the town.

Stagecoach Group were latecomers for the versatile Optare Solo. Compare the doorway and accessibility of this bus with that in the previous picture. Well suited to its daily duties, it is loading at Bridge Street for another circuit on 8 March 2010. Banbury Town Hall can be seen behind the bus. When Coventry DVLA office closed, new Midland Red South vehicles received Northampton-registered plates as the head office was based at Rugby depot.

The depot extended back from the original Canal Street buildings and housed a wash road and engineering facilities. The Dennis Dart with Plaxton Pointer bodywork had matured to become this clean-styled low-floor vehicle, then badged as Transbus Dart. Stagecoach Group operated nearly a thousand across the UK on a variety of work. Originally at Oxford, 34469 (KV53 NHD) was one of seven transferred to Banbury and on 7 November 2009 the bus had completed a day's work on route 59 (previously X59 and now Gold S4) serving Oxford. The oval-shaped plate just visible over the air inlet on the front panel was applied when new to display branding for route X4, Oxford to Abingdon. (Raymond Bedford)

Geoff Amos was an established operator based in the rural Northamptonshire village of Eydon. Their coach fleet contained some interesting marques, the majority bought new. One of a pair of Bova Europas new in March 1982 XAM 116A (previously ENH 44X), numbered 48, wears the older colour scheme when seen operating a private hire at Buckingham Palace Road, Victoria. (R. Eversden/Author's collection)

Amos' main bus operation was a service between Banbury and Rugby loosely following the route of the long since closed Great Central Railway. Wadham Stringer-bodied Dennis Dorchesters once plied the route but Rural Bus Grant funding in 2000 allowed for extra journeys to be added and new low-floor vehicles joined the fleet. A batch of MCV Evolution-bodied MANs were received in 2005 for the service which was numbered GA01/GA02. At Banbury on 8 March 2010 53 (AM05 BUS) is ready to head back to Rugby. The company closed in 2011 and this bus would go on to work for Faresaver in Chippenham.

New in 1977, Midland Red South 606 looks resplendent in the pre-Stagecoach Western Travel rocket red, white and grey livery. Another Leyland National to be repowered with the distinctive sounding DAF engine, a day out to the North Weald bus rally was being enjoyed in this June 1990 view. This Rugby-based vehicle saw use in the Centro area, as evidenced by the windscreen sticker, with an Almex ticket machine in view as well. This equipment was also used by associated company Cheltenham & Gloucester. (Author's collection)

Having made a cautious trip to Northampton on route 88 from Rugby, DAF-powered Leyland National 629 (PUK 629R) lays over on Victoria Street on the last day of 1996. This main route, the predecessor of which was the X96, was altered in 1999 with First Northampton running the service. The Mounts police and fire stations dominate the backdrop and this street is now classified as Northampton's coach station. Rugby's Leyland Nationals soldiered on until 2000.

First Northampton broke free from their traditional borough boundary operating area to run the group of routes towards Rugby under council tender. Initially terminating at the village of Crick, the Rugby link was later re-established and at North Street in that town on 8 May 2008 Plaxton Verde-bodied Dennis Lance 67204 (L204 AAB) heads towards home. New to Midland Red West, this type was in use at Northampton towards the end of their operations and had replaced newer low-floor vehicles. Stagecoach once again runs the route, now numbered 96.

Stagecoach in Warwickshire commenced route 72 between Rugby and Daventry in 2009. The hourly service had two branded vehicles, one of which was 34133 (V133 MVX) a Dennis Dart SLF with Plaxton Pointer 2 bodywork new to the Group's East London operations. Taking a slightly different route to Geoff Amos, the service number had origins with Midland Red's 572 and was a good link between the Warwickshire and Northamptonshire operations, which were at the time separate. At Dunchurch on 8 March 2010 a United Counties NBC-era bus stop flag is attached to the same pole as the Geoff Amos timetable case.

National Express and Megabus Operations

Stagecoach Group established Megabus in August 2003 on a route from Oxford to London. Along the same lines as budget airlines, tickets were purchased via the internet and started from £1. Former Hong Kong Leyland Olympians were initially used with nearly seventy re-imported to the UK in 2003/4. Some received private plates or UK marks from their depots' local DVLA office. Leyton depot (T) were allocated seven of the type. 13607 (J703 HMY, EW 9215) works the Birmingham route at Priory Queensway. Toilets were fitted to some of these vehicles. (Author's collection)

With most National Express contracts withdrawn by 2005, the vehicles used on such work were re-deployed on Megabus duties. Carrying smart Jonckheere Mistral bodywork Volvo B10M 52623 (S903 CCD) was new as East Kent 8903 for the National Express Dover to London service. Several of this type were allocated to Rugby where their Megabus diagrams would take them to all corners of the UK. At Birmingham International railway station on 23 June 2009 a pair work a special hire for Virgin Trains, then jointly owned by the Stagecoach Group. The coach was later re-registered 456 CLT.

It was emphasised to local depots that, no matter what, Megabus services must run and this lead to some interesting substitutions or duplicates during busy periods. Plaxton Premiere Interurban-bodied Volvo B10M 52285 (283 URB, N145 XSA) was from Cowdenbeath depot's 'Joint Venture' pool. Captured at Newton Street in Birmingham on 29 June 2009 the coach would work a mid-morning journey to London. Its registration mark is now carried on a preserved Chesterfield Transport Leyland Tiger.

Preston depot would often provide a vehicle from their own local coach allocation, 52614 (S270 KHG) being such an example. Several of these Jonckheere Modulo-bodied Volvo B10Ms were delivered to the Group circa 1998. On 30 June 2009 a crew change is taking place at Watford Gap services.

Despite what is shown on its branding, not all routes would go in and out of London as cross-country links were being established. The M34 ran between Portsmouth and a variety of destinations in the north, in this case Bradford. On 12 February 2011 Jonckheere Mistral-bodied Volvo B12M 52677 (FN04 JZR) was loading at Oxford's Water Eaton P&R site at 08:05. The vehicle was acquired with the Yorkshire Traction Group and previously carried the registration 1901 HE when in service with them on National Express contracts. It would later receive another identity, 670 CLT, when working for Rennies of Dunfermline.

Scotland to London coach services formed part of Stagecoach's pioneering operations based in Perth. These would later be provided under the Megabus brand with even a 'gold standard' sleeper facility offered. Neoplan and Van Hool Astromega double-deck coaches were used on these extremely popular routes. Tow bars were fitted to the vehicles and passengers' luggage would be accommodated in the trailer. A significant number of drivers required their licence to be upgraded in order to pilot such vehicles. For a while Warwickshire's training coach 52358 (P158 ASA) spent as much time in reverse as it did in forward gear. Another driver is put through his paces on 23 January 2009 at Long Marston airfield. The site is now a housing estate; is the bollarded 'garage' now a real one?

The central geographic area featured in this book is advantageous to coach operators as four-and-a-half driving hours could take you to numerous towns and cities including a range of coastal resorts. Family-run Catteralls Coaches, based in the Warwickshire town of Southam, was a National Express contractor. One of forty similar vehicles new to Parks of Hamilton, FHS 746X is a Duple Goldliner-bodied Volvo B10M. Simple National Express fleet names are applied, including non-standard 'Rapide' lettering, and the company name is boldly displayed at the front as it heads through Dunstable on the A5. The coach went on to work for Pathfinder, Newark. (Kevin Lane/Author's collection)

Midland Red South was involved with six National Express routes at the time of this 4 March 2003 view depicting the longest example, route 337, which ran from Rugby to Paignton. Departing at 11:20 from the latter, Rugby would be reached by 19:40. Advertised fares for an adult were £33 single, £44 return. 52436 (R36 AKV) was originally numbered 36 and would go on to work the X5 route from Bedford depot. This was the final NBC-style livery application which also featured an internet address, signalling the dawn of a new era. (Author's collection)

Arriva Midlands and Arriva MK Metro jointly operated a number of National Express contracts from 2007. The wheelchair-accessible Caetano Levante was introduced to the network from 2006, coupled to Scania or Volvo chassis in two- or three-axle configurations. Its lines are shown on 0422 (FJ09 DXO), a Scania example. Departing on time from Clifton Road, Rugby, at 08:20 on 24 June 2010 its ultimate destination of Brixham was scheduled at 17:20, which included an hour break at Bristol. The route was lost in July 2014 to South Gloucestershire Bus & Coach, the vehicle going on to work for Eirebus in Dublin registered 09-D-124951.

With other companies operating frequent services between Oxford city and London, National Express decided to pursue opportunities using the new M40, with route 420 being such an example. This ran to a frequency of roughly every sixty minutes between London and several destinations in the South and West Midlands. From 2004 luxury was introduced to the network in the shape of the Irizar Century PB which featured leather seats as standard. From National Express's own fleet, NXL3 (YN04 GXU) of Digbeth depot stands beside West Drayton-based NXL15 (YN05 WJA) showing support for Birmingham's Irish community. Body styling differences can be observed in this 14 February 2010 view on Elizabeth Street, Victoria, part of which was closed for road works.

Coventry, Leamington and Stratford-Upon-Avon

Moving on to Coventry, at the old Pool Meadow bus station in July 1992 Midland Red South 416 (J416 PRW) loads for Nuneaton. One of eighteen Wright-bodied Mercedes-Benz 811Ds, the thirty-three seats offered almost midibus capacity. The name of the bus reflects the area's industrial past, and is one of six named after local pits. (Author's collection)

The majestic sounding Pool Meadow consisted of several rows of drive-through bays, with the original concrete bus shelters replaced with slightly more modern structures. G&G Travel of Leamington Spa was part of the Western Travel Group and ran a very varied fleet. Two Leyland Lynxes were delivered new in 1988 and mainly used on routes to Leamington Spa. Carrying a local overall advert in this July 1992 view, F661 PWK would carry fleet numbers 111 then 819. Transferred to Ribble in 2000 the bus was later sold to Blazefield's Burnley & Pendle subsidiary, with a final move to Bus Eireann as LS118 (88-D-43621) in 2003.

The Regency architecture of Royal Leamington Spa provides a backdrop for buses loading at Upper Parade. Towards the start of this book we saw Stagecoach's early influence at Oxford with double-deck deliveries. By 2006, after use at Witney depot, the Volvo Olympians moved to Warwickshire. Now all to single-door configuration some received this bold livery for use on services serving the University of Warwick. 16514 (R414 XFC) works such a duty on 8 March 2010. Later receiving the majority red-based Unibus livery the vehicle operated from several Stagecoach Midlands depots including Northampton.

Pool Meadow was refurbished in 1994 becoming a much more pleasant and comfortable facility, with its nineteen departure bays arranged in a 'w' shape if viewed from above. A range of operators utilised it, with Travel Coventry by far the most frequent, as depicted in this 8 May 2008 scene detailing three of the company's common types. An Alexander ALX400-bodied Dennis Trident loads on the stand with a late model MCW Metrobus Mk 2 soldiering on past wearing the old livery variation. An integral Mercedes-Benz 0405N lays over in the company of M.J. De Courcey vehicles.

From 1998 Travel West Midlands (TWM) received almost 200 Mercedes-Benz 0405Ns, which were used across the whole operating area. Twenty-one of these were articulated. Joining the ten Coventry had received new were examples transferred from Birmingham including 6003 (T603 MDA), which had been used on route 67. The driver makes a careful study of his mirror while departing Pool Meadow on 8 May 2008.

Founded in 1972 by Mike De Courcey, M.J. De Courcey Travel ran services in and around the Coventry area with a National Express coach operation featuring in later years. Several West Midlands operators prefixed their names with 'Travel' in similar style to TWM. A range of interesting vehicles have featured in the fleet including Alexander TE-bodied Leyland Tiger MJI 2368, new to Eastern National as HHJ 378Y. Coventry's Broadgate is festively decorated on 3 November 1997 as the bus passes through on the two-hourly 775 service from Nuneaton. (Author's collection)

De Courcey entered the low-floor era in 1997 with a number of types being used. Proving a popular combination with independent operators was the Egyptian-built MCV Evolution with MAN chassis. 553 (AE55 VGM) was one of a number in use by De Courcey and was loading on Trinity Street, Coventry, on 8 May 2008 working commercially operated route 22, which competed with similar TWM route 21. Several of the batch would go on to work with Faresaver in Chippenham from 2013, and De Courcey ceased operation in August 2020.

TWM's Coventry depot in Ford Street is a stone's throw from Pool Meadow. In 2008 a sizeable number of MCW Metrobus Mk 2s were still allocated there, with most of the company's 600 examples overhauled by Marshall of Cambridge. Coventry's version of corporate livery and corresponding fleet names adorn 3001 (F301 XOF) at Trinity Street on 10 June 2008, with few takers for its destination of Tile Hill. The last TWM Metrobuses ran in July 2010.

In equally large numbers with TWM was the Alexander ALX400-bodied Dennis Trident, as exemplified by 4397 (BV52 OBM). Seen working Travel Coventry route 12, which operated at a frequency of up to every ten minutes, the bus was loading at Upper Parade in Leamington Spa on 8 March 2010. University students form a large part of the passenger traffic between Coventry, Leamington and Sydenham.

Based in Binley, to the east of Coventry, Haywood & Prosser traded as A-Line Travel. A bus operation ran alongside the coach business with route 101 running into home territory. Smartly presented Alexander Dash-bodied Volvo B6 L652 OWY came from Harrogate & District, and loads on Trinity Street on 10 June 2008. Today A-Line specialises in coach operations.

TWM's Coventry depot didn't operate services on New Year's Day so a series of routes was put out to tender by Centro. Stagecoach Warwickshire won these exclusively for several years and ran the operation from Nuneaton, utilising drivers from all local depots. At Broad Lane, Banner Lane terminus, Transbus Pointer Dart 34496 (KV53 NHN) waits to return to the city centre on the first day of 2009. In 2010 services were also operated by Travel De Courcey.

In 2007, Stagecoach Group launched the Goldline brand in Perth with full-size single-deckers, and in Leamington with Optare Solos. To 'woo the middle classes', Solos with twenty-seven leather-covered coach seats operated on route G1 (previously numbered 66) to Warwick. 47511 (KX57 KGG) loads on Upper Parade in the royal spa town on 8 March 2010. The bus would later receive corporate livery when reallocated to Northampton depot. Leamington depot was the recipient of the Group's first batch of Solos in 2001.

During the NBC era Midland Red received a number of ECW-bodied Leyland Olympians, the 'south' division taking fourteen from new. A pair delivered in October 1984, with seventy-two dual-purpose seats, wore NBC 'Venetian blind' coach livery. However, this would not last long as under Western Travel ownership Stratford-based vehicles received this blue version of fleet livery and 'Stratford Blue' fleet names, recalling operations of a previous generation. 961 (B961 ODU), named *Dorothy*, was definitely heading to Alcester in July 1992 when viewed at Bridge Street in its home town. Sold to GHA of Ruabon in November 2002, the bus was scrapped in April 2012. (Author's collection)

A member of Stagecoach Group's special event fleet, AEC Routemaster JJD 565D arrived through acquisition of Ensignbus's Stratford-upon-Avon operations in February 2007. RML 2565 also carried corporate identity 12565 and had previously been used by Stagecoach's East London division before being sold to Ensignbus in 2003. On 3 June 2010 it was seen at Compton Verney House operating a special service.

In February 1999 Stagecoach Midland Red received its first new double-deckers since the ECW-bodied Leyland Olympians, with eight Alexander RL-bodied Volvo Olympians being delivered to Leamington depot. 16616 (S916 ANH), previously numbered 916, was still in use from the same depot when this 19 November 2008 view was recorded at Bridge Street. Wearing the distinctive Unibus livery while working hourly route 26 to Redditch, its colour scheme would blend in well with that of First Midland Red's 'Barbie' vehicles.

Playing a significant role in Warwickshire's bus operation was Johnsons of Henley-in-Arden. Their modern bus fleet was smartly turned out in a bright yellow and blue colour scheme. A little different was Optare Solo YN53 YHA, liveried for Stratford-Upon-Avon park and ride, caught on camera on 20 November 2008 while picking up on a festive looking Bridge Street.

Johnsons offered an extensive tour and excursion programme with coaches also seen across the region on private hire and contract work. The company had a liking for Bova with this 1995 Futura example, M10 RGJ, seen on Dudley Street coach stand in Birmingham on 19 November 2008. Styling of this Dutch product altered little over the years. The van behind is about to enter the Bull Ring loading bay, previously the entrance to the gloomy bus station, long since closed.

West Midlands Links

TWM operated route X20 between Birmingham and Stratford-upon-Avon. Journeys were hourly on Sundays and bank holidays during the summer months, and every two hours in winter. 4021 (T421 UON), based at Birmingham Central depot, was one of TWM's twenty-two low-floor Optare Spectras. Its capacity was certainly needed on 3 May 1999 at Bridge Street, Stratford, where it was conveying day trippers back to the city.

The principal hourly service X20 was provided for many years by Midland Red South. The route was sponsored by Warwickshire County Council under their 'County Links' scheme, which included the supply of vehicles to the contract provider. A trio of early production Alexander Dennis Enviro 300s was initially allocated to Pete's Travel, then to Stratford Blue when the contract changed hands. SN04 EFR was numbered 403 when the company was taken over by Stagecoach in 2007. That group also operated vehicles of this early design in the north-east and in Winchester. By now carrying 'national series' fleet number 27504 in this view on Wood Street, Stratford, on 20 November 2008, the destination is set for its next journey. Johnsons now run the route with double-deckers branded 'The Bards Bus'.

Substituting for an Enviro-300 on 19 November 2008 was Alexander PS-bodied Volvo B10M 20225, previously based at Rugby branded for route 86. It is standing on Moor Street, between the modern architecture of the Bull Ring shopping centre and the heritage styling of Moor Street railway station (which included a steam engine), before heading back to Stratford-upon-Avon. A greater number of bus stops now occupy both sides of the road.

'Diamond' was used as a brand name by the Birmingham Coach Company for its bus services that principally served the Black Country. In December 2005 Go-Ahead bought the operation. It was joined in March 2006 by Pete's Travel (later People's Express) becoming Go West Midlands and placed under the control of COMS. The Diamond brand name was retained and an influx of step-entrance and low-floor vehicles from other Group companies soon followed. Plaxton Pointer-bodied Dennis Dart SLF 497 (R461 LGH) was one of a number from London and was allocated to Tividale depot. Loading in the city centre for Druids Heath on 19 November 2008, it is working route 50, which competed with the high-frequency TWM service of the same number.

Go-Ahead Group sold the West Midlands operation to the Rotala Group in March 2008. With over a hundred vehicles acquired the new owners were very dynamic in their reorganisation of the business, introducing new vehicles and launching distinct branding. Redditch area operations were 'Red Diamond', the livery perhaps a nod to Midland Red. New to Thames Travel as 351 in 2001, Mini-Pointer Dennis Dart 519 (KP51 UFC) had just received a fresh coat of paint and was returning to Redditch on 21 August 2008. Later transferred to Tividale depot, repainted into 'Black Diamond' livery and renumbered 20519, the vehicle was eventually scrapped in 2018.

One Careful Owner

South Midland was sold to its management in December 1986, operating as such until December 1988 when bought-out by Transit Holdings. Around a hundred vehicles were acquired with nearly all conventional types soon withdrawn, including forty-six ECW-bodied Bristol VRs. Most wore striking liveries and branding, an example of which is still carried on coach-seated TBW 452P when seen at Southend in 1991 with its new owner, Stephensons of Rochford. The bus would later see service with Classic Coaches of High Wycombe. (Author's collection)

An ECW family likeness can be appreciated on these vehicles operated by Emblings, and exhibited at Sacrewell Farm, Peterborough, on 5 July 2009. The Bristol VR on the left once wore the same South Midland livery as in the previous image and from 1988 had worked for a number of East Anglian operators. Named *Deirdre* the vehicle is now in preservation with Eastern Bus Enthusiasts. Its stablemate is NNO 66P, a Leyland Atlantean named *Lily-May*, which was new to Colchester Borough Transport.

Vanguard was part of the Western Travel Group. It ran buses and coaches but also had a dealership side of the business, the stock of which included a pair of ex-COMS ECW-bodied Leyland Leopards, still wearing South Midland 'Orbiter' livery. Having been pressed into service alongside numerous other Leopards of differing origin, VUD 32X (VUD 28X parked behind) was seen at the company's Bedworth yard in December 1990. The fleet was absorbed into the parent Midland Red South operation later taken over by Stagecoach Group. (Author's collection)

Joining several Bristol VRs working for Roselyn of St Blazey, was this Oxfordshire duo. This established Cornish coach operator had taken AEC Bridgemasters and Regent Vs from COMS and the Atomic Energy Research Establishment (AERE) in the 1970s, for bus and contract work. At the end of the following decade Bristol VRs took their place from the same sources. Ex-AERE XAN 48T carried an overall advert for a DIY chain's local branch. Former COMS 495 (HUD 495W) was one of a pair acquired from Crosville Cymru (as DVG495), after the Welsh company had obtained them with the purchase of the Devaway business. An overall advert was later applied to the Oxford Bus Company base livery. The pair are pictured at Roselyn's depot on 16 June 2001. (Author's collection)

Even minibuses would feature on the second-hand market. Stevenson's of Uttoxeter ran an incredibly varied fleet and expanded its operating area largely through opportunities presented by privatisation. Quirky names featured on minibus networks and C727 JJO has gone from a 'Nipper' to a 'Pacer'. One of eleven long-wheelbase Ford Transits with twenty-seat Carlyle bodies acquired from COMS in 1991, they would run together with a batch of ex-SYPTE Dennis Dominos in Stockport. Seen at that town's bus station in September 1992, 221 is still wearing its previous owner's colours. (Author's collection)

Gloria Glide had retired from P&R duties in 1996 although part of her image is still visible below the head of the elderly lady passenger by the time Mellor Duet-bodied Iveco 2040 (L321 BOD) had passed to Newcastle-Upon-Tyne based North Rider. Numbered 23, it joined other Iveco minibuses in the fleet while retaining its middle door. A none-too-helpful destination features in this August 1996 view. (Author's collection)

Seen at Twickenham Stadium on 20 April 2002, for a Northampton Saints vs London Irish match, 52022 and 52023 (L157 and 158 LBW) were from East London's Romford North Street depot coaching unit, where they were numbered VJ9 and VJ8 respectively. Having already had careers on the Oxford Tube, Stagecoach Express X5 (Cambridge–Oxford) and X6 (Peterborough–Stansted), the duo still look smart. After further use at other Stagecoach depots, both were reunited and operated with Roselyn Coaches in Cornwall from 2015.

Stagecoach Group swapped most of the dual-door Dennis Darts based in Oxford for East London's single-door examples. Seen on Gale Street, Dagenham, on 23 October 1999, PD68 (M68 VJO) leads an older 'L' registered stablemate. Their livery was uninspiring but complied wholeheartedly with the Transport for London rule that all buses should be painted red. The low-floor era, soon to come, would see the former Oxford vehicles move on again to a number of Stagecoach Group depots.

A visit to Cairns, Australia, brought something of a familiar feel when passing by one of the central area bus stands. Sunbus was part of the Transit Australia Group that Harry Blundred OBE had established in 1995. The layout of 252b (048 DPP), a Mercedes-Benz with dual-door Custom Coaches body, conforms with the Transit Holdings minibus specification as it waits along with similar vehicles in the summer sunshine on 5 February 2008. The location looks somewhat more tropical then either Oxford or Exeter's High Streets.

High mileages were soon accumulated by vehicles working the intensive London and airport services. Four new Plaxton Premiere 350-bodied Volvo B10Ms, from dealer stock, entered service on the X90 in November 1997 with cherished 'OXF' registration plates. All were withdrawn by April 2003 when the batch was re-registered for further use within the Go-Ahead Group at Wilts & Dorset. Three out of the four carried this smart livery for the new X33 route between Bournemouth and Southampton. Previously numbered 2 (R2 OXF) at Oxford, 3235 with its new identity R813 NUD loads at Bournemouth Square on 16 June 2004. The route was short lived and the vehicle would soon transfer to Salisbury, and then to Southern Vectis on the Isle of Wight. It lastly saw service with Notts & Derby. (Author's collection)

We see again a member of London Buses' one-time VN-class VN8 (K8 KLL), which assumed the identity 651 at Oxford with registration K125 BUD. In late 2005 ten of the batch moved to Southampton where they were converted to single door by Solent Blue Line at Eastleigh. By 2011 this particular vehicle had been chosen by Southern Vectis for a unique reconfiguration. Following an earlier generation of interesting conversions for IOW seaside routes, the rear roof section was cut away and the windows were removed. Complete with new livery, it was branded the 'Shanklin Steamer' for a circular route around that town once performed by Dotto land-trains. However, its use was short-lived and it moved on to its fifth and final owner, the Isle of Wight Bus Museum, where it now forms part of the static collection and doubles as the café's seating area. On 18 September 2011, 625 was spotted on the mainland while attending the annual Showbus rally at Duxford.